WHERE THE RUBBER MEETS THE ROAD

WHERE THE RUBBER MEETS THE ROAD

Thirty Essential Tips for Counsel
to Best Serve Their Clients

NATE R. BOHLANDER, ESQ.

ILLUMIFY
MEDIA.COM

Where the
RUBBER
meets
THE ROAD

Published by
Illumify Media Global
www.IllumifyMedia.com
"Let's bring your book to life!"

Paperback ISBN: 978-1-959099-84-0

Typeset by Art Innovation (http://artinnovations.in/)
Cover design by Debbie Lewis

Printed in the United States of America

For Finley,
who completely changed my life
the first time she looked up at me.

Contents

Acknowledgments

Thank you to my parents. In navigating my own adventure in fatherhood, I have come to appreciate your constant sacrifices and support for me more each day. There wasn't ever a day I didn't feel unconditionally and completely loved, and that's a debt I can never repay.

Thank you to my wife. I wouldn't be able to dive headfirst into a project like authoring my first book if not for your support. By demonstrating strength and conviction, you make me want to be a better husband and father each day.

Thank you to Bella and Leila. Caring for you prepared me to care for my daughter. Plus, you helped me fall in love with her mother.

Thank you to my friends, many of whom I've known for the better part of three decades. It brings me such comfort to know that no matter if we're celebrating or commiserating, we'll always be a call, drive, or flight away, even on very short notice, wherever and whenever we're needed.

Thank you to my colleagues, coaches, and mentors, both academically and professionally, including my teachers and coaches at Wyoming Seminary, my professors at Dickinson College and Penn State Law, and my employers and coworkers throughout my post-education career. I've learned so much about myself and the world around me by being challenged and guided along the way.

This book, and hopefully a few others in the future, wouldn't be possible without all of your influence on my life and help in getting through it.

Introduction

*F*rom the moment I started to drive, my dad began teaching me about keeping my car in good shape. He naturally wanted me to keep the oil changed, the fluids topped-off, and all that good stuff. But the one thing he always checked on *personally* was my tires.

One day, after I inquired about this practice, he told me why.

When I was very young, Dad worked as a volunteer fireman and paramedic, and reported to the scenes of many accidents. Time after time, he would arrive at a location where a driver had run off the road and hit a tree, collided with another car, or something of that nature. He said that in almost every case, the tires were, or were very close to, bald. He told me that no matter how fancy all the gizmos and gadgets in your car, the only things hitting the road are the tires.

It's a lesson I never forgot. And really, it's a lesson that goes beyond vehicle safety. It's about always remembering what's most important. It's literally "Where the rubber meets the road."

We get so caught up with all the bells and whistles of things. For a car, we find it easy to focus on the horsepower, the enhanced technological features, and all the other *sexy* features that are accentuated in advertisements. But for any car, the priority should always be the tires.

For an attorney, it's the client. *The client is the priority.* Not any portion of the case itself.

But far too often, we forget that. I know that I have.

Indulge me while I tattle on my own profession for a moment. To put it kindly, we attorneys can be a bit self-absorbed, even though we don't necessarily intend it. We worked hard to graduate law school and pass the bar, and yes, we should take a little pride in that. And while the practice of law can appear boring for some, for us it can be exciting. Particularly in the realm of litigation. We get a case, and we immediately start planning how to win it. We bury our noses in research, begin writing, strategizing, and filing motions – all the fun stuff that lawyers tend to do. Of course, we absolutely need to complete all these tasks. But somewhere along the way, we forget about the very people and entities *for whom we are doing those very things.*

In practicing as a civil defense attorney for a decade, I can't recall how many times I've seen the scenario where assigned counsel gets handed a case, immediately starts working, says to himself/herself, "I know how to win this," and spends multiple thousands (or even tens of thousands) filing and arguing a multitude of motions over several months.

Then, comes back to the client with, "Sorry, we lost. Here's your bill."

Here are some questions to consider:

- Did counsel explain to the client the odds of success? Probably not.

- Did the attorney inform or provide a draft of all the filings? Not likely.
- Did counsel provide timely progress reports? Counsel was too busy.
- Did the attorney give the option of approving or declining certain expenses? Doubtful.
- Did the client notice these things hadn't happened when they were handed the bill?

You bet they did.

I've heard the feedback from clients about other attorneys time and time again: "Why didn't we know about this?" "We didn't approve this." "Why didn't the attorney do thus and so instead?"

In absolutely *zero* situations does this end well. So why does it happen so often?

To borrow the metaphor from my dad: attorneys forget to check the tires.

I'm not saying we as attorneys are not doing our jobs, or even that we're not doing our jobs well. Many of us excel in things like developing case strategies, making compelling arguments, lowering the value of cases and so on. But things like client communication, following client directives, client satisfaction, putting the client's needs and wants first . . . we're not always very good at those. *But we can be with just a few slight changes to the way we practice.*

That's really the inspiration behind this book: the belief that we as counsel can, and should, do better with respect to servicing our clients.

In my experience, we can learn in three ways. We can *learn from our own mistakes*; we can *learn from the mistakes of others*; and we can *learn by heeding sage advice* from people we trust. Each of the thirty tips in the following pages comes from one or more of these sources. Sometimes, I'm sharing lessons learned from my own personal experience. Other times, it's something I learned by observing someone else's mistake and how the client responded to it. And sometimes, even though I've never observed the issue, it's a key nugget of advice gleaned from one of my mentors that has paid off for me.

Since I've observed that the number one pitfall with attorney-client relationships is poor communication, many of these tips are geared toward client reporting, including when to report, what to report, how often to report, and so on. But there are other things, too, like owning our mistakes, going the extra mile, being forthright in delivering bad news, and not being afraid to be personable. But each tip boils down to answering one basic question: *How can we, as attorneys, better serve our clients?*

This book focuses on three audiences: attorneys, clients, and any related individuals and entities, such as claims handlers. For clients and claims handlers who read this book, my hope is that the curtain will be peeled back a bit, in order to see a little deeper into our processes, and so that you will know what you can and should expect – and yes, even demand – from us as attorneys.

For fellow attorneys, especially those hired as assigned counsel, my hope is that you will engage in a bit of self-reflection, find value in these tips, and strengthen your relationships with your clients so you can continue to do great work for them.

After all, the attorney-client relationship is truly where the rubber meets the road.

TIP 1

Never Bury the Lede

"*I*t was a bright cold day in April, and the clocks were striking thirteen."

With this famous opening line from the novel *1984*, a work which seems to grow in relevance with each passing day, author George Orwell wastes no time in conveying that things may not be what they appear, urging readers to maintain a skeptical mindset as they delve further into the story.

As assigned outside counsel, we should employ the same tactic when reporting on our cases. I'm not talking about setting a similarly ominous tone. I'm talking about the writing technique of engaging the reader from the very first line and letting them know what the report is about.

Journalistic writing follows a similar rule of conveying the most important information at the top of the article, mainly because they expect most readers won't read all the way to the end. In fact, it's rule number one, and therefore it's my first tip: **Never bury the lede.**

WHAT IS THE LEDE?

In journalism, the lede refers to the opening section of a news story, designed to grab the reader's attention and provide the most important information of who, what, when, where and why upfront. The lede aims to engage the reader and entice them to continue reading the rest of the piece. The phrase "burying the lede" refers to hiding those relevant pieces of information deeper within the article. While creative writers and novelists, like Orwell, do this to pique the reader's interest, journalists also use this tactic because readers may not dig into a news article unless they recognize the topic from the outset.

Indeed, the nature of litigation often involves periods of downtime, sometimes lasting weeks or even months. During those times, our reports are understandably brief and relatively uninteresting. I've written, "In the interim, we will otherwise stand down in all material respects" more than a few times in my career.

But what about those times when counsel needs to report on significant events such as completion of depositions or newly acquired medical records? Or if we are requesting authority to retain experts or engage in settlement discussions? When major case events occur, especially those that directly and substantially impact litigation strategy or valuation, unfortunately, many attorneys stick to a repetitive script. They start with an overview of the facts, you know, the same facts that existed for two years prior to initiation of the suit and another several months or years in active litigation. Then they move on to procedural history, such as when the complaint was filed, the allegations against our client, and the details of responsive pleading. In other words, they provide the same information that's been reported a multitude of times already. All this comes before actually bringing up what *this particular report* is about.

If that's not burying the lede, I don't know what is.

Instead of following the same old script for each report, we should focus on addressing the following questions: What crucial information does our client want and need to know right from the outset? And how can we deliver this information in both the most effective and efficient manner possible?

Common sense says we should put this information at the *top* of the report, rather than hide it somewhere in the middle. So, for example, if the plaintiff's deposition took place, the information gleaned should be right at the top of page one. The same goes for judicial decisions on our submissions, bombshell discovery responses, and any other new development that has taken place since the last report.

A HELPFUL TECHNIQUE

Here's the good news. As attorneys, we don't have to learn to be journalists to better inform our clients via our reporting. We don't have to change our writing style completely. To enhance the clarity and conciseness of my reports, I often implement either underlined takeaways or bullet points at the beginning of each report. These points highlight the key essential information that the client needs to know, even if the rest of the report goes unread.

And here's the trick. I add the bullet points after I've drafted the substantive report itself.

Here's my technique:

- I draft the report as usual, in my own writing style.
- When the report is finished, I review it and make notes. I ask myself, "If the report were a game, what parts of it would make it onto *SportsCenter?*"
- Then, I go back and add those important bits as bullet points at the top of the report.

This approach does two things for the client. It not only gives them a quick snapshot of the case up front, but also a roadmap of what can be expected over the next few paragraphs or pages. That way, even if they skim the report, they still have a good idea of what is happening.

Considering that we must report some degree of inane and repetitive material in our cases, the last thing we need to do is bury the lede or pertinent information that our clients really need to know. We don't have to be George Orwell to capture their interest. We just need to know where to put, and how to highlight, the information to make sure they see it.

So next time you draft a report, emphasize crucial information, use bullet points for clarity, and ensure that your reports are both informative and straightforward. Keep the reader's needs and expectations at the forefront.

In other words, let the clock strike thirteen right off the bat.

TIP 2

Know the Rules of Engagement

*N*o doubt about it, settlement negotiations can be tricky beasts.

To start with, there's the counsel posturing that invariably happens at the beginning of negotiations. Added to that is the timing. (Yes, it's true, cases are more likely to settle on Fridays, particularly before Holiday weekends.) And obviously, there's the question of the amount of the settlement itself.

Ironically, it seems like the biggest hurdle to a successful settlement negotiation can be figuring out the intricacies of the settlement terms; specifically, your client's requirements. Many settlement talks fall apart over technicalities that should have been discussed up front but weren't raised until the release was reviewed. When this happens, at best, the settlement is delayed, and, at worst, the case becomes litigious.

I learned this lesson early in my career when I jumped into a settlement negotiation prematurely, without having a clear understanding of what my client would accept, and the conditions under which they would accept it. Thankfully, after the "song and dance" of both sides threatening judicial involvement, it all worked out, and, after wiping the egg off my face, I took the lesson to heart.

You must **know the rules of engagement** so you can truly serve your client. You must know your client's directives *before* starting settlement negotiations.

WHAT WE NEED TO KNOW

It's a simple concept, really, but one that is often missed. We are so focused on the back-and-forth that happens between opposing counsel that we overlook the fact that before we even pick up the phone, we need to be armed with two vital pieces of information.

First, the offer we're authorized by the client to make; and second, the non-negotiable terms and conditions – or deal-breakers – of any prospective settlement.

Knowing What You're Authorized to Offer

The actual amount of an offer is fairly straightforward. What sum is your client willing to pay to the plaintiffs and their attorneys? Then, again, the dollar figure is never just a number. For instance, it can be tied to other facets of the settlement. For example, your client may agree to a specific contribution only if another co-defendant matches it. Alternatively, you might only be authorized to propose an offer if the plaintiff's counsel absorbs the mediation costs. You should know these details up front.

Knowing the Terms and Conditions

Then there are the broader contours of the settlement agreement, the stuff that doesn't necessarily have to do with money but is still just as important. For example, Is confidentiality of the settlement terms, or a non-disparagement clause, a material piece of the agreement? Can payment be rendered to plaintiff's counsel in forty-five instead of thirty days? Must all produced confidential materials be destroyed, and an affidavit produced to that effect? Has it been made clear that all liens are the responsibility of the releasor?

By getting these types of questions answered with your client before beginning settlement negotiations, you can head off any surprises and ensure the process goes smoothly. And ultimately, that will get to the result everybody wants, a swift and successful resolution. It's a simple matter of not putting the cart before the horse. Before you enter the battlefield of settlement negotiations, make sure the rules of engagement are crystal clear.

TIP 3

If You Don't A-S-K, You Don't G-E-T

*A*fter graduating college, I went to work for a non-profit organization. I found the work fulfilling and I was passionate for the cause, but fundraising always made me uneasy. The task of soliciting donations felt daunting to me, often causing me anxiety as potential donor meetings approached.

On one particular day, I found myself in the car with my boss, heading toward a meeting with a repeat benefactor. As usual, I was a bundle of nerves, contrasting sharply with my boss who was cool as a cucumber. I asked him how he managed to stay so calm during these interactions.

He turned to me and shared a piece of wisdom that has stuck with me since: **"Hey, if you don't A-S-K, you don't G-E-T."**

His meaning was simple yet profound. no matter how uncomfortable the "ask" may be, the organization for which we worked relied on donations, and we couldn't do our jobs unless these folks agreed with our vision. The temporary discomfort of simply asking paled in comparison to the potential long-term detriment to our cause (and our personal careers) if the funds did not arrive.

WHY WE NEED TO ASK

Attorneys, I believe, can and should apply this principle in client reporting. You might find this hard to believe, but counsel is often reluctant to ask for things that cost money, for example, retaining experts, traveling for onsite meetings or inspections, conducting depositions of third parties, subpoenaing treatment records, or contributing to a global settlement offer. The rationale is that, since we're already billing the client an hourly rate for our work, asking for additional expenditures beyond that might upset them.

But do you know what's *worse?* Foregoing these requests just because they are uncomfortable, when we have a real chance at saving the client money on the backend.

Yes, hiring an expert might require an upfront investment, but the insights derived from their report could potentially dismantle the plaintiff's liability claims. Likewise, contributing to a global settlement might mean writing a check now, but it could result in significant savings in future litigation costs and help avoid a damaging verdict later.

As attorneys, part of our duty involves gauging the entire landscape of a case and determining the best course of action for our clients. This could mean that the client must pay some extra costs upfront in exchange for additional resources that can potentially turn the tide in our client's favor.

Sometimes, that means taking the initiative to A-S-K.

After all, that's the only way to G-E-T.

TIP 4

Act Like You've Been There Before

*M*y dad, who was a college professor for over four decades, recently retired. He and I have enjoyed watching Steelers games together since I was very little. During these games, he often expressed his frustration with the players who celebrate every minor victory; for example, treating a sack on first down as though they had single-handedly won the Super Bowl.

One day, I asked him, "Why do you feel so strongly about players celebrating on the field?"

"When I finish a good lecture, do I dance down the hallways?" he replied.

While his answer initially took me by surprise, it actually made a lot of sense. He was basically saying that a professional should always remain composed and maintain their dignity, even in the midst of success. Treat that success as though it is to be expected. It's not the first time it's happened, and it won't – or at least shouldn't – be the last.

In other words, **Act like you've been there before.**

Counsel should embrace this mindset in client reporting.

SHARE THE WINS, BUT DON'T TOUT THEM

To take pride in your case achievements is natural, and indeed necessary, whether your triumphs are procedural or investigatory breakthroughs. In many situations, having a motion granted or uncovering a crucial fact via creative discovery requests can dramatically reduce the value of a case, sometimes even leading to its complete dismissal. Those types of wins are indeed cause for celebration, and obviously, you should put those developments front-and-center of the very next client report.

However, attorneys must resist the urge to pat themselves on the back when conveying this information to the client. Not only is it self-aggrandizing, which is not a great trait to exhibit, but it also suggests to the client that these types of triumphs are few and far between. This could lead to an unnecessary concern on the part of the client, which is not the perception attorneys want their clients to have.

KEEP THE CLIENT'S BANDWIDTH IN MIND

Consider that the person reading the report likely has a multitude of other claims to deal with, some of which may be occupying more of their mental space than yours. If that's the case, an over-enthusiastic celebration could come off as slightly tone-deaf at best, and transparently juvenile at worst.

Therefore, while it's important to enumerate the positive development in detail and briefly explain why this outcome is beneficial for the client, it's equally crucial to maintain a level-headed approach. In essence, the key is to reflect an air of seasoned experience rather than novice excitement.

Act like you've been here before. Share the victory, then move on.

TIP 5

Stop Trying to Impress Them

*W*hat goes through the minds of clients when they receive case status reports from their lawyers, filled to the brim with complex legalese? The famous line from Shania Twain springs to mind: "That don't impress me much."

Lawyers are renowned, and often mocked, for their inclination to complicate language every chance they get. Given the choice of expressing a point in multiple ways, they invariably opt for the most grandiloquent approach. Do you see what I did there?

But why is this tendency so prevalent in the legal profession?

Because we believe that we need to demonstrate a complete mastery of the English language?

- Because we need to prove our worth to the reader?
- Because we think we bill by the word?
- This brings me to my next tip: **Stop trying to impress the client.**

Here's the cold, hard truth. All the flowery legal language we put in these reports doesn't accomplish the goal of impressing the reader. All it does is frustrate and annoy them.

Our clients know that we went to law school. They know we passed the bar exam. They know that, if we really put our minds to it, we could ensure that every other word in a report is Latin. But why would we do that? Does that help the goal of the report, which is to convey and analyze crucial developments in a case in a way the client can understand?

Of course not.

Consider a simple scenario where the court grants our motion. A lawyer might choose to report this development to the client as follows: "After consideration of the respective positions of counsel, as set forth not only in the filed motion and opposition, but also oral argument, the court rendered a decision with respect to same, ordering that the requested relief prayed for therein be granted."

Come on. We've all done it.

But here's another way of putting it: "The court granted our motion."

Sure, the first version has some great words. "Therein" is one of my favorites. We might even throw in a "thereon," "thereto," or "heretofore" if we're feeling a bit cheeky.

But the second version is infinitely easier and quicker to digest. And isn't that the point?

YOUR CLIENT IS ALREADY CONVINCED

It's not our job to impress the client. It's our job to *communicate* with them. And that means using language that is clear, concise, and honestly accessible. I'm not saying to "dumb it down." My clients are some of the smartest people around. Just don't go too far in the other direction and pull out the thesaurus for every word.

Don't worry. Your client knows you're bright. That's why they hired you. You don't need to waste precious ink convincing them. Just tell them what they need to know. *That's* what will impress them.

TIP 6

Be More than
Just a Reporter

The way in which Americans consume their news, or should we say, are *fed* their news, has undergone a profound transformation over the past few decades.

It used to be that the news programs had a mere thirty minutes per night to tell us what was going on in the world. Sixty years ago, at the end of that half hour, Walter Cronkite would end with the catchphrase "And that's the way it is." Because, in large part, that's the way it was.

Edward Murrow. David Brinkley. Tom Brokaw. Barbara Walters. Peter Jennings. The list goes on. The common thread was that these anchors, each with different personalities, objectively relayed the facts, and then the program just . . . ended. There was no roundtable discussion. There were no "pundits" to break everything down for us. There were no transparent ideologues relaying their personal, or political party's, positions. Reports consisted of one truthful, declarative statement after another.

Not so much anymore.

The advent of the twenty-four-hour news cycle has increased pressure to make news more interesting and keep a viewer's attention. Now, every media outlet provides an in-depth analysis of each story, oftentimes via a split screen of four to eight individuals becoming increasingly determined to prove that they are the . . . loudest?

This trend is undeniably irksome. Like so many of us, I wish we could go back to the "boring" version of the news. Leave the analysis up to us in our own homes. It might actually do us some good and calm us down a bit as a society. But ironically, when it comes to attorneys reporting to their clients, I have the *opposite* opinion. I think we can learn something from today's more expanded version of the news, and I think it's an approach attorneys should adopt. Which brings me to my next tip: **Be more than just a reporter.**

INTERPRET AND EXPLAIN FOR THE CLIENT

When we think of an attorney's report to a client, it should be much more than just a recounting of events. Clients aren't looking for a scribe simply to take notes on what happened. They're looking for interpretation, insight, and guidance on how those events could impact their case.

The questions a client may have from a development in a case can be numerous and complex. Here are some of them.

- Does this development necessitate a fundamental change in strategy?
- Is there a need to adjust reserves?

- What are a particular motion's chances of success?
- Should we consider additional depositions or third-party record retention?
- Do we need to engage an expert?
- Would it be prudent to propose a settlement?
- If we follow a particular strategy, how might the opposition respond?

THE KEY IS SEEING THE FACTS FROM MULTIPLE SIDES

All these critical considerations don't exist in isolation. They need to be contextualized and analyzed. The client needs to see a development from multiple sides to make informed choices about what's next.

Imagine what a report would look like if an attorney wrote: "Plaintiff's counsel has repeatedly requested that we engage in mediation," without adding anything about what counsel's insistence may mean with respect to "striking while the iron's hot."

In another situation, what if the assigned counsel reported that the plaintiff's discovery responses included a past and future wage loss claim but did not follow up with any analysis about potentially retaining a vocational or economic expert.

Being an attorney goes beyond just reporting. Analysis is also a fundamental part of the job. By adopting a more analytical approach, akin to modern news outlets, attorneys can provide their clients with a deeper understanding of their situation and more valuable advice for their cases. But we can certainly do so in a far less bombastic manner than the network talking heads.

TIP 7

Take Off Those Rose-Colored Glasses

*T*hink about the saga of *Star Wars*. In teaching his young protege the ways of the Force, Obi-Wan Kenobi once gave Luke Skywalker this key piece of advice: "Your eyes can deceive you, don't trust them."

"Life lessons from *Star Wars*?" you ask. There is arguably no better source! In fact, it certainly won't be the last such reference in this book.

While Obi-Wan was trying to get Luke to trust his feelings over what he actually saw, there's a takeaway in this saying for us as well. We all have this tendency to see what we want to see in the world. We subconsciously construct our desired outcomes, and then we trick ourselves into believing that this result, which was essentially willed into existence, is now fact. Something like a self-fulfilling prophecy.

Take us attorneys, for example. We're often so engrossed in our cases that we know each intricacy like the back of our hands. When formulating arguments, we fully embody them, having spent, in many cases, *years* immersed in extensive research about the related issues. We exude a natural sense of confidence as we prepare to draft the brief, or deliver the oral argument, of the century.

However, therein lies a potential pitfall. We can get so consumed by our case that we lose the ability to maintain complete objectivity about our chances. That false sense of confidence can slightly mislead our client at best and be overtly costly to them at worst.

That's why I say **Take off the rose-colored glasses.**

HAVING A REALISTIC VIEW

As attorneys, we are skilled at crafting good-faith arguments in nearly every circumstance. We have been trained that way. We can make almost anything seem logical. But just because it makes perfect sense to us doesn't mean that a judge or jury will feel the same way. Nor does it mean our opponent can't poke enough holes in our position that our filing begins to look like Swiss cheese.

It's crucial to remember that a winning argument in one venue may falter in another, and victory today doesn't guarantee success tomorrow. Unforeseen developments must be accounted for, and every conceivable outcome anticipated.

To stay ahead of the game, we need to think outside the box and prepare for all possible outcomes. And that means stepping back and seeing things how they are, with respect to both the positives and the negatives. We need to look past what we want and evaluate the situation with an objective and realistic eye.

Even if we've got every fact and facet of the case committed to memory.

GIVING THE CLIENT A CLEARER PERSPECTIVE

Taking off the rose-colored glasses isn't just for our benefit. Just as importantly, this information needs to be conveyed to the client truthfully and without bias so they can be prepared for all outcomes. We can do this by practicing the following:

- **Transparency**: Always be upfront and honest about the potential outcomes of a case, even if it's not what the client wants to hear.
- **Clarity**: Clearly explain the reasons behind your expectations. Break down complex legal jargon into terms your client can easily digest.
- **Balance**: While it's important to maintain optimism, balance it with realism. Don't over-promise or create false hope.
- **Context**: Provide context for your predictions. Explain any relevant legal standards and how they might impact the case.
- **Updates**: Keep your client updated on any changes in the case that could alter the expected outcome.
- **Contingency Planning**: Discuss possible setbacks and how you plan to handle them. This ensures your client is prepared for any situation.

Granted, it's annoying to have to write to the client: "Despite having a very strong argument on the merits, considering the jurisdiction, we do not anticipate that our motion will be successful. "

But I submit that this is still better than having to write: "Despite our prior report anticipating that our motion would be granted, the court inexplicably denied it."

So, the next time you are about to report that the client is headed for an easy victory, remember Obi-Wan's sage advice: "Your eyes can deceive you."

TIP 8

Availability Is the Best Ability

*F*amed NFL coach Bill Parcells was known for his quips. I'm stealing one of his most memorable sayings, and my personal favorite, for my next tip: **Availability is the best ability.**

Coach Parcells was making the point that of all the characteristics a football player can possess, including size, speed, toughness, and intelligence, the most important one is availability to play on Sundays. To Coach Parcells, being there for one's teammates to help win the game was paramount over all else.

Attorneys should heed these words of advice when reporting to their clients.

BEING AT THE CLIENT'S DISPOSAL

Reports can become overwhelmingly complicated in a hurry, especially when several significant developments have occurred since counsel's last interaction with the client. Not only do these case events often require extensive explanation, but the subsequent formulation of litigation strategies based on these events can be even more intricate. If all the client has is the written report, they're likely to get lost in all the analysis, explanation, and strategic suggestion.

Sometimes, it's just better to clear things up with a phone call. That's why, at the end of almost all my reports, I include the line "Please contact me with any questions or concerns." I always want to signal that I am at the client's disposal.

That I'm *available*. At *their* convenience and on *their* time.

THE SIMPLE ADVANTAGES OF A PHONE CALL

When a report includes more complex topics, or when a major strategic decision needs to be made, I go beyond simply making myself available for a phone call. Instead, I *suggest* it. You'd be surprised at how efficiently and effectively you and your client can work together when you're communicating verbally. Here's why:

- *A phone conversation is faster than email.* You can bring the client to understanding more quickly and effectively.
- *A phone conversation allows for extra-verbal signals.* Both parties can glean information from the other person's tonality, voice inflection, and other characteristics that would remain a mystery via email. This also improves overall communication.
- *A phone conversation is live.* As your dialogue raises additional questions, you can answer them in real-time versus days of email exchanges.

- *The client appreciates the high-touch effort.* It shows that you're invested in the success of their case.

So the next time you report to your clients, remember Coach Parcells' advice and offer them your most valuable characteristic: your availability.

TIP 9

It Depends

*A*h yes, every attorney's favorite phrase.

This answer has been my go-to response for a myriad of legal inquiries since I first graduated from law school. My family and friends would often bombard me with an array of legal questions, and more often than not, my answer was simply: **"It depends."**

THE LAW IS COMPLICATED

The law is not as cut-and-dried, or black-and-white, as most people might assume. Instead, it's a complex tapestry of nuances, exceptions, and conditional clauses. Every so-called hard-and-fast rule comes with its own set of exceptions, and a single minor detail can completely alter the trajectory of a case. As frustrating as it was to utter "it depends" repeatedly to those seeking my informal legal advice, it was the only honest way to respond to their queries.

It has been more than a decade since I graduated from law school, and the phrase still holds true, especially when it comes to providing verdict and settlement valuations to clients.

Our firm has a policy in place where we deliver a comprehensive litigation strategy report, at the very latest, within the first forty-five days of receiving a file. Oftentimes, this report is provided much quicker than that. This report includes a crucial piece of information integral to the overall litigation strategy: the estimated valuation.

The valuation can significantly influence our client's directives. For instance, if we tell a client we expect a jury verdict award in the seven figures, their reaction and subsequent directive will likely be different than if we told the client we were expecting a verdict in the four figures. The same principle applies to potential settlement values.

Given the importance of these valuations, we invest a significant amount of time and resources into their preparation. This involves, among other tasks, meticulous analysis of medical, employment, and financial records, conducting thorough online searches of the plaintiff, investigating the incident alongside our client, subpoenaing providers, submitting right-to-know requests, assessing the venue and assigned judge, evaluating opposing counsel, calculating liens, and researching verdicts in comparable cases.

However, even with such rigorous preparation, we cannot ascertain some facts yet because there are just too many variables, for example:

- The plaintiff's likeability is largely gleaned from their deposition.
- Additional co-defendants may be joined in the matter.

- The case's venue may not yet be set.
- Discovery responses and/or document production have not yet been received.
- An onsite, in-person inspection has not been conducted.
- Court decisions on motions have not yet been made.
- Liability and damages consultants and experts may either enhance or undercut our defenses.

Considering these uncertainties that typically emerge in the early stages of a case, providing a single figure or even a fixed range of figures may not sufficiently inform the client about potential exposure. "It depends" is simply the most useful phrase to describe such cases.

TWO RANGES

Due to these variables, over the past few years, I've adopted a practice of offering two ranges each for potential jury verdict and settlement values. Each range is based not only on the information available at the time of the report, but also considers potential future developments that could move the needle. For instance, if we successfully move the case to federal court, one range applies. If not, we anticipate a verdict or settlement within the other range.

By providing multiple valuation ranges, complete with the factors and analysis that underpin them, clients are better equipped to understand and prepare for what lies ahead. While it would be ideal to provide clients with a definitive answer to their exposure question at the very outset of a case, the reality of legal practice often necessitates the most common of all attorney replies: "It depends."

It's frustrating. But it's also honest. And that's what our clients need.

TIP 10

Give Them the Movie Version

*I*t's a classic sitcom plot. A kid gets assigned a book report for some literary classic, let's say, *To Kill a Mockingbird*. (Hey, I'm a lawyer. What did you expect?) Instead of reading the book, the kid goes to the theater and watches the movie to write his report.

Or have you ever asked someone if they read a particular book, and their reply was, "No, but I saw the movie"?

It feels like cheating, but in many ways, it's not. We naturally gravitate to visuals because they communicate more quickly (two hours of watching versus twenty hours of reading) and effectively provide imagery versus calling on imagination. We respond more vividly to what we see than what we read. What's the saying? "A picture is worth a thousand words."

This principle can be quite useful in our reporting, as well. This leads me to my next tip: When communicating information to your client, **give them the movie version**.

Here's another illustration of what I mean. What kind of social media post most easily captures your attention? Is it

- A long, wordy post with lots of descriptive text?
- Or one which conveys that same point by using engaging imagery?

Even more to the point, Which option takes the least amount of time to convey the most information? Which one does so more effectively?

The way you feel while scrolling through wordy social media posts is exactly how your client feels when they're reading through your comprehensive case reports. They'd much rather *see* what you're describing than *read* about it.

SO WHENEVER POSSIBLE, DON'T TELL THEM. SHOW THEM.

Allow me to play "Captain Obvious" for a moment. Consider the following:

- Every incident occurs in a specific location or a series of locations.
- Every incident involves some sort of action or activity.
- Most incidents leading to personal injury claims entail individuals suffering bodily harm.

That's actually a lot to communicate. The incident that gives rise to your case is a crucial event that needs to be communicated to your client accurately and thoroughly. What's the best way for defense counsel to do this? *By using pictures.*

In other words, the movie version.

WORTH A THOUSAND WORDS

Have you ever tried to read through a lengthy, multi-paragraph description of an incident? It can be quite a challenge. Now, imagine being presented with a clear photograph of the incident scene, complete with diagrams showing the locations of individuals, the purportedly injurious mechanisms, and other relevant details. Much, much easier to digest, right?

The same principle applies when discussing damages. Take, for example, a degloving injury. This can be communicated in a report either through a detailed textual explanation or by including a photograph of the plaintiff. The impact of such photographs can be incredibly powerful. After all, except in very limited circumstances, the jury will eventually see it, so why not let your client see it now?

Granted, some people prefer reading books over watching movies because they enjoy using their imagination. They don't want the exact appearance of Gandalf easily delivered to them; they'd rather form their own image based on pages of J. R. R. Tolkien's descriptive text.

But that's not your client. You need to assume your client, who may receive ten other substantive reports today and is juggling hundreds of matters, is the visual type.

They don't want to read a book. They want the movie version.

So, give it to them.

TIP 11

Sleep On It

I dare say it happens to the best of us.

On many occasions, I have found myself on the receiving end of a rather, shall we say, "terse" email from opposing counsel. The content was riddled with inaccuracies, misquotes, and thinly veiled threats. Provocative, to say the least.

Naturally, without fail, my initial reaction has been to hit "Reply" and begin feverishly crafting a response, delving into the case's evidentiary record for backup. However, every time I've received one of these emails, and each time I've started on my reply, I've stopped. A piece of sage advice came drifting into my mind, advice given to me more than once by individuals far wiser than me: "Before hitting the 'Send' button, **sleep on it.**"

In other words, take the time to fully analyze things. Evaluate all potential outcomes of your actions. Let boiling emotions settle. In short, wait at least one overnight before taking any further action.

I close my laptop. The following morning, I reach out to the opposing counsel directly, questioning the need for such an aggressive email, and stating my position on the topic at issue.

Almost always, we've managed to resolve our differences in short order.

SLOWING IT DOWN

This principle, I believe, holds true in most of our interactions as attorneys, even in client reporting (when we're not likely to be in a state of heightened emotion). After all, "sleeping on it" doesn't just refer to diffusing our irritation. It also refers to slowing down and staying methodical.

When it comes to something as vital as client reports, it's crucial to take the necessary time to ensure absolute accuracy. Although it might be satisfying to quickly send the email and move on to another task, our primary objective should always be the complete, accurate, thoughtful, and efficient communication of facts and analysis. Is rushing a report really conducive to achieving this goal?

Of course not.

So, if you complete a comprehensive report in the late afternoon, maybe after a deposition or receipt of a judicial decision on your motion earlier that day, and there are no exigencies that require immediate action, hold on to it. Give it one more night. Review it with your morning coffee. If you spot even a single typo, minor misstatement, formatting error, omitted detail, or realize you could have used a slightly different tone, you'll realize the wait was worth it.

Your client deserves nothing but your best. So, give it one more sleep to ensure you deliver just that.

Don't Be Mr. Roboto

*M*y wife and I were driving through the Catskills on our honeymoon when Styx's "Mr. Roboto" came on the radio.

Without any hesitation, I cranked up the volume, singing along with fervor and even breaking into a spontaneous robot dance during the final chorus. (Warning: Do not attempt this while driving in the mountains.) With a triumphant declaration of "I am Kilroy!," I turned to my new bride, eager for her opinion of my rendition of this classic tune.

She looked at me and, in a deadpan tone, said: "That's absolutely the worst thing I've ever heard."

In the interim, I've somehow gotten over the disappointment. In part because she clarified that it was the original song, and not my added vocal, that was so displeasurable to her. I'll give her the fact that it's not a song for everyone.

While I may be unable to contain unbridled excitement about the prospect of a song about a humanized robot, client reporting requires a different approach. That leads me to the next tip: **Don't be Mr. Roboto.**

TAKING A MORE HUMAN APPROACH

The law may be emotionless, but humans are not. That's why, when reporting to our clients, we attorneys need to get past the "machination" of the law, and instead display an emotional side. Here are some practical ways to do so.

Present case facts with compassion.

When you present a narrative of the matter, it's crucial to demonstrate empathy, especially regarding the severity of damages. You should be able to step away from your role as a staunch representative and consider the emotional impact. For instance, if defending a case involving a young plaintiff with severe facial scarring, it's not necessary to downplay the injury throughout the report. You will certainly attempt to lessen the injury's value at trial via, among other avenues, expert testimony and reports. However, even though you're representing the defendant, dehumanizing the incident will make you seem cold, and possibly create a subtle loss of respect.

Use a conversational tone.

An attorney should aim to communicate case developments in a conversational tone, providing analysis while maintaining a friendly rapport with the client. For example, do clients want to read like this?

"The judge to which our pending motion was assigned is somewhat unlikely to deliver a favorable outcome, given Her Honor's perceived propensity for denying similar motions in the past."

Okay, maybe some of them would like it written that way. But it's far more likely they'd appreciate a straightforward, casual style. Something like the following.

"We have been before the judge to whom our motion has been assigned previously. While we find Her Honor to be fair, always greeting litigants with a friendly quip, she is not particularly fond of granting complete dismissals at this stage, so we should cautiously prepare for a denial."

See how that's a bit more accessible?

Establish a personal connection with the client.

Don't be afraid to befriend your client. Check in with them about life events you've shared. You're both human beings first, and professionals second. During calls with established clients, I routinely ask about how they and their families are doing before we delve into business. Clients always appreciate the gesture and reciprocate it by asking questions of their own. This brief personal interaction (unbilled of course) sets a warm and caring tone for our conversation and reinforces our relationship.

So, as you prepare your next client report, remember the famous song from Styx's "Mr. Roboto"? We are not robots without emotions, so allow your humanity to shine through in your work.

TIP 13

Stay in Your Lane

$\mathcal{A}$t first glance, the tripartite relationship between client, carrier, and counsel may seem uncomplicated. The client, having paid premiums, receives insurance coverage from the carrier. In turn, the carrier remunerates the attorney for her time to defend the client against any claims brought against them. It's a seemingly clear-cut arrangement, with well-defined roles for each party involved.

Yet, sometimes this simplicity becomes clouded. Resultantly, attorneys may find themselves on the precipice of overstepping their professional boundaries.

Simply put: Don't do that. If uncertainty arises, it's always better to fall on the side of discretion — sealing your lips and ceasing your pen.

In other words, **Stay in your lane.**

A plethora of case elements fall outside an attorney's jurisdiction, for example:

- While you can – and should – provide anticipated pure exposure and settlement ranges, refrain from

pontificating on how much should be paid to
resolve the matter.

- Don't comment on where the carrier should set
reserves.
- Stay away from the carrier's decision on tender.
- Avoid making suggestions to the client about their
standard operating procedures (SOPs), training,
manufacturing, testing, or other internal processes.
(You can offer to do that after the matter concludes
as part of a new arrangement, but not while the
case is pending).
- Keep your commentary about the client's
employees' actions to yourself.

OUR LANE IS CLEAR

As the attorney assigned to the case, your role is crystal
clear. You're tasked with representing the client, analyzing the
claims, investigating the facts, applying them to pertinent laws,
strengthening defenses, mitigating damages, and lowering
valuation of the claim.

Take note that none of these responsibilities intersect with
the prohibited actions mentioned earlier.

That said, there may be instances where our input is expressly
sought. For example, we might find carriers asking us at a
mediation whether a case should be settled for a specific amount.
Similarly, clients may seek our opinions as to how their internal
policies and procedures in place at the time of the incident may
impact the liability analysis.

In such scenarios, we may cautiously and gently step outside our usual role. But remember, unless explicitly asked, it's best to leave the turn signal alone.

TIP 14

Show Your Work

*R*emember those notorious "show your work" prompts on grade school math tests?

The process goes a bit like this: You're confronted with a mathematical equation, and you're certain you've arrived at the correct answer. Eager to move on to the next problem, you see the dreaded instruction: "Show your work!"

What?! Why does that matter? The answer's correct and that's the whole point!

Of course, it's not *just* about the final answer. The teacher needs to see that you've mastered the process required to reach the solution. This principle also rings true when it comes to providing pure exposure and expected settlement values in client reporting. So my next tip is **Show your work**.

MORE THAN JUST A NUMBER

As I mentioned in a previous tip, within the first month or so of receipt of a file, we draft a comprehensive litigation evaluation for our clients. We incorporate anticipated figures into these plans to avoid surprises toward the end of a case, which allows the clients to brace themselves for various potential outcomes. Ultimately, we provide a range (or set of ranges) for both pure exposure/jury verdict and settlement values. They are conspicuously highlighted and are the focal point of the section.

However, these figures are not pulled out of thin air; they are the result of a thorough, multi-faceted examination of every conceivable factor that could sway liability and damages. To get to these numbers, we research, among a host of other elements, including:

- Past jury verdicts in cases with similar facts in the same venue;
- Potential social inflation;
- Jury breakdown;
- Court (and, if applicable, assigned judge);
- Anticipated rulings on motions throughout discovery; and
- The impact of deposition testimony.

We don't simply provide a figure; we map out the journey taken to arrive there. This ensures the client is aware of all the considerations that went into the final product, and that every possible angle was evaluated. Additionally, we maintain any relevant jury verdict research results for the case. We've been asked for these before, especially when an anticipated exposure value exceeds the clients' initial expectations, and it is best to supply them to validate the calculations.

Yes, the final answer is undeniably the highlight. However, when you are being paid to provide it, and counted on to get it right, you must show your work.

TIP 15

Use the Identification Number

I think the term "customer service line" is a misnomer. Perhaps "customer torture line" would be more accurate.

After the multi-hour elevator music serenade, you may eventually speak to an actual human being. Should you be so lucky, what is the very first question that you are always asked?

I'd venture to guess that it is some version of "May I have your identification / customer / order number please?"

Before anyone will even listen to your concern, you need to provide some means by which you and your order can be located in their system. This will allow the customer service agent to bring up all pertinent information, so they can communicate in the most efficient possible way.

The same is true in the world of client reporting. **Use the identification number**.

WHICH CASE ARE WE TALKING ABOUT?

Attorneys pride themselves on drafting comprehensive, informative, and downright compelling reports. They hit that

"Send" button and can't wait for their client to be so impressed that they question why they ever retained any other counsel. There's just one problem, the subject line of the email, or heading of the document, didn't include the claim or docket number.

You know, the only way to identify which matter the report involves.

Put yourself in the shoes of a client or claims handler who works with a bevy of attorneys on hundreds of open claims. Imagine receiving a correspondence that dives straight into a deposition summary without any identifying information. It's bound to leave you feeling overwhelmed and confused, spending precious minutes trying to locate the plaintiff's name so that you can pull up the case and comprehend the report.

MAKE IT EASY FOR THEM

There's an unbelievably simple fix to this. When sending a report, *use the identification number.*

Include the carrier's claim number upfront.

Better yet, include the carrier's claim number *and* the court's docket number.

Better yet, include the carrier's claim number, the court's docket number, *and* the date of loss.

By incorporating these identifiers, you ensure that the recipients can easily locate and analyze the information, regardless of how they choose to look it up. This makes for a smoother, more efficient communication process overall.

Why make your client's life more difficult? What takes you mere seconds on the front end saves them precious minutes down the road.

TIP 16

Fall on Your Sword

*I*n the time of ancient Rome, after a particularly unexpected or embarrassing loss in battle, soldiers would often choose to end their own lives by impaling themselves on their swords. They believed that death was a more desirable alternative to living with the shame of defeat. Although this act has mercifully vanished with the passage of time, the phrase has survived, and is now used metaphorically to express acceptance of blame for an unfavorable event.

This concept appears to be one that we in the legal profession are especially reluctant to embrace. For various reasons, it seems attorneys often struggle with acknowledging our mistakes to clients.

- Perhaps we think that we are truly infallible.
- Maybe we honestly don't think we were at fault.
- We could believe that, once we apologize, the malpractice police will come for us.
- We fear that the client will fire us.

Any of these could apply, of course. However, in my experience, when the attorney steps forward, explains the situation, accepts responsibility, and offers remedial solutions, clients tend to respond not just with understanding, but also appreciation.

Which is why I say, **Fall on your sword.**

A PERSONAL EXAMPLE

I recall an instance where a client and I were engaged in a flurry of emails discussing numerous pressing issues. Among these was the topic of proposed redactions to a document before it was to be shared with all parties to a case. In one of these emails, the client expressed her approval. I misconstrued this to be her agreement with the redacted document, while she was actually referring to another item concurrently being discussed in the same set of emails.

When she requested to review the document once more before its distribution, I had to admit that it had already been sent out. I immediately apologized for the misunderstanding and suggested several possible solutions. Fortunately, the redactions were minor and didn't cause any harm. Despite the mix-up, my transparency and swift apology were well-received.

MISTAKES ARE INEVITABLE

They are a part of human nature, as unavoidable as death and taxes. Rather than evading them and hoping they go unnoticed, it's better to confront them head-on, the moment they happen.

It is vital to have the difficult conversation and find a way to fix them.

If you make a mistake, and you're absolutely going to, there's no need to emulate the Romans and literally fall on your sword. But perhaps a figurative *dive* toward your keyboard or telephone might be in order.

TIP 17

Check Back In

*O*ur golden retriever, Leila, has an adorable trait. Ever since she was young, whenever we walk her without a leash, she periodically runs back to my wife and me and just stares at us. It's as if she is performing a self-imposed roll call check-in. This behavior wasn't instigated by us calling her back, nor is it a result of any particular training. There's no treat waiting for her. She just does it on her own. She has seemingly made the choice on her own to check in with her parents occasionally as if to reassure herself—and us—that she is doing the right thing and all is well.

Counsel can take a page from Leila's book.

It serves as an important life lesson, especially in my role as an attorney. It leads to my next nugget of advice: **Check back in.**

In the legal profession, we are often so engrossed in the specifics of our cases that we tend to overlook the bigger picture. Our interactions with clients are mainly centered around the claims or cases at hand, with discussions mainly focused on different strategic elements that could potentially sway the case in our favor. Each call is pointed and direct. There is a clear goal between us to achieve the desired outcome in the most efficient manner possible. But I also think there is immense value in fostering broader communication, meaning engaging in conversations that aren't strictly dictated by a predetermined checklist or agenda. Here's why I think this helps:

- It establishes a more human connection (see previous tip);
- It's a way to build rapport and trust with the client; and
- It provides an opportunity for personal growth.

Once every year, typically around the holiday season, I make a point to reconnect with all my clients. There's no claim or case to talk about. There are no reports or updates. I am not requesting authority to retain an expert or subpoena additional depositions. Instead, I just want to wish my clients happy holidays and thank them for my continued trust in me. I also invite them to provide candid feedback and constructive criticism. The only objectives of these calls are to take time away from *work* to let them know that I care about our relationship and ask them how I can improve my representation of their interests and become a better attorney in the future. I find these conversations are as beneficial for me as they are for the client.

THE BOTTOM LINE, IT HELPS US GET BETTER AT WHAT WE DO.

Much like our beloved Leila, sometimes it's essential to pause, turn back, and check in with our clients, ensuring that everything is as good with them as it can possibly be. The importance of maintaining a strong relationship cannot be overstated. Whether the conversations result in the validation that we're on the correct path, or whether we learn of ways to improve our representation of clients' interests, this practice of checking in is a valuable one that can help us become better attorneys in the long run.

TIP 18

Use All Available Resources

During the many delightful years my wife and I spent living in Center City, Philadelphia, I genuinely enjoyed going to the dentist.

Yes, you read that right. No, I'm not a glutton for punishment. Not only was she a great practitioner, but we shared lots of laughs.

She was blunt with her assessment of my oral health, and I absolutely loved it. Every time she would tell me my teeth looked good, I would respond with a silly comment like, "Hey now, look at me!" She would reply with something like, "They look good *for now*. Keep brushing." Ah, those were the days.

When we moved, I had to find a new dentist. Not something I wanted to do, but certainly reasonable and necessary.

My strategy in doing so was twofold: conducting online research and seeking personal recommendations. In addition to looking up dentists' ratings, websites, and locations online, I asked around for recommendations. Many of my family members and friends are local, so I knew there would be a bevy of opinions out there.

Most of us tend to use a similar approach whenever we need to make significant purchases or hire services. For example, would you ever contemplate buying a car or hiring a realtor without consulting your trusted inner circle? Probably not.

Then it raises the question: Why do we, as attorneys, readily apply this method in our personal lives but often overlook it in our professional endeavors?

Hence, my next tip: **Use all available resources.**

GOING THE EXTRA MILE

At the start of a new case, assigned counsel should provide to the client a comprehensive analysis of the assigned judge, opposing counsel, and other factors influencing valuation. Many attorneys naturally resort to online research, scouring Google, social media platforms, and legal research sites for information. However, this approach lacks invaluable personal knowledge that can only be gained through connections.

We're not using *all* available resources; rather, just the easy, convenient ones.

This is where we should go beyond standard investigation. Reaching out to colleagues should be a given, but it's also beneficial to consult contacts at other firms as well. In my own practice, these steps have uncovered some exceptionally helpful tidbits.

Maybe a plaintiff's attorney tends to posture unreasonably right up to the time of trial only to fold and accept the last conveyed offer.

Maybe a judge has a soft spot for a certain line of argument or a particular penchant for granting certain motions.

These aren't insights you get from online reviews or writeups. These insights come from asking around; by *using all available resources*. And it's the little things like this that can move the needle, even slightly, in our client's favor.

As assigned counsel, our mission is to gather every piece of information possible to defend our client effectively. If we seek personal references and opinions when choosing a new dentist, shouldn't we do the same when analyzing someone who will stand as our opposing counsel or render dispositions in our case over the next few months or years?

Keep Asking for Directives

A few years ago, I really wanted to bring my wife pancakes in bed for her first Mother's Day.

I had it all planned. I got up early, got our daughter set up with her favorite morning time food of bananas, and began working on breakfast. But despite my meticulous attention to detail, the pancakes stubbornly clung to the pan, refusing to cooperate. I had been careful with my measurements, used wife-approved coconut oil, and didn't overcook them. Yet, success eluded me.

Awakened by the burning smell, my wife came downstairs, and, witnessing my struggle, quietly entered the kitchen. Even though I had been certain I was doing things the right way, my results spoke for themselves. I knew it was time to seek guidance from the true master of our kitchen. She pointed out that the pan I was using, although seemingly identical to another I always use, was not the right one for pancakes.

This experience taught me a valuable lesson: never blindly follow a path, especially when expert advice is within reach. In other words, **Keep asking for directives.**

DO SO EVEN IF YOU'RE ALREADY ON A PARTICULAR PATH.

This principle applies not only in the kitchen but also in attorney-client relationships and client reporting. Attorneys often enjoy considerable latitude in shaping and executing day-to-day strategies. Propounding discovery, serving subpoenas, and at least initiating discussions about potential resolution typically fall under the attorney's purview. However, this autonomy doesn't negate the importance of seeking client directives, even if a specific course has already been set.

For example, if you've received discovery responses or document production from another party that are clearly deficient, you may believe that a discovery deficiency letter is the best route forward, followed by a motion (if necessary). Yet, your client might not see the value in pursuing this information given the associated costs. Similarly, you may believe that the plaintiffs' inflated demand doesn't warrant a response, let alone an invitation to discuss a settlement. But if your client wants to start that process, trusting that opposing counsel will "come to their senses" in the face of a reasonable offer, they have the unfettered ability to make that decision.

DEFERRING TO THE CLIENT

You may be an expert in legal matters, but remember, the client is the master of the kitchen, er, case. No matter how confident you are that you're using the right pan, they've got the right to ask (and ultimately tell) you to use a different one. All it takes to keep the client informed while involving them in the decision-making process is as simple as one line in a report: "If you would like me to take a different course of action, please let me know."

That single line shows complete deference to your client. And that's as it should be.

TIP 20

Be a No-Man

When one individual is employed by another, there's an inherent risk of becoming a yes-man to the one in power. We see this dynamic across the professional world, especially since most of us interact with bosses or clients. Maybe you've observed a few yes-men in your time. You know, those folks who are agreeable to the ends of the Earth in an attempt to please those for whom they work.

Maybe you've even been one. (Gasp!)

The one who holds the power dictates the workflow and remuneration, and therefore, being a yes-man might seem like a surefire way to maintain job security and avoid conflict. However, this approach has its downsides. Primarily, it may result in subpar service since it inhibits open dialogue and constructive criticism.

Consider the relationship between attorneys and their clients. As counsel, we want to please our clients. We also want to get paid, and we definitely do *not* want to get fired. But the yes-man approach is not in our client's best interests, which is why I say, **Be a no-man.**

We largely take our marching orders, and field questions, from our clients. They determine, among other things, whether to file suit in the first place, whether to demand or offer particular amounts to resolve a case, whether to file particular motions, and whether to take a case to trial. Our clients also make numerous *requests* of us throughout the pendency of litigation. Things like whether we can avoid a particular deposition.

Inevitably, there will be occasions when clients ask their counsel if it is possible to take steps that run afoul of the rules (usually unintentionally, but rather just from a minor misunderstanding of how things work in a particular venue). These, above all else, are times to be a no-man.

A PERSONAL EXAMPLE

Luckily, none of my clients have ever directed or knowingly asked me to do anything improper. But I have had the undesirable job of saying "no" to more than one client.

I remember having a client who, after sharing numerous materials with me in advance of document production, questioned the necessity of disclosing a particular set in discovery. While these documents weren't overwhelmingly detrimental to our defense, they certainly didn't strengthen it either. I exhaustively considered all possible reasons for not producing these materials. However, they were relevant, responsive, and not privileged or protected in any way.

The call to my client wasn't all that fun. I was the epitome of a no-man, as in, "No, we can't withhold those records." The alternative would have been to breach my ethical duty just to appease my client, and I certainly wasn't going to do that.

Thankfully, my client was understanding. We disclosed the documents and managed the minimal fallout that ensued.

It's undoubtedly tough to be a no-man. The conversation might be a bit awkward and tense.

But it's also unequivocally necessary. It's an indispensable part of maintaining professional integrity.

Don't Hide
Behind the Keyboard

These days, it seems like we are more disconnected from one another than ever.

Yes, the pandemic forced us into relative isolation out of necessity. But that doesn't explain why we haven't really reconnected since. And, indeed, this process slowly began happening before the pandemic.

It appears that some of this disconnect has been by choice. And, of course, made much easier by technology.

Social media platforms and messaging apps have become an integral part of our daily lives. From Snapchat to Instagram to WhatsApp, these digital tools have overtaken traditional means of communication such as face-to-face interaction or phone calls. Nowadays, it's not uncommon to be asked *why* someone could have *possibly* decided to make a call rather than just send a text.

This shift toward digital communication is particularly noticeable when it comes to discussing contentious topics or delivering unfavorable news. Our computer keyboards enable us to drop a piece of negative information and simply walk away. With no discussion in real time, there's less of a chance that an argument or admonishment will ensue.

We've all witnessed instances where teenagers end relationships via text messages, or even more shockingly, managers terminating employees through emails. But is this the most effective way to communicate about such significant matters?

As attorneys, we frequently encounter situations that will negatively impact our clients. Whether it's a corporate deposition gone awry, a court denying a critical motion, or the unearthing of an unexpected liability, these scenarios demand more than just a comprehensive report followed by a polite "please call with any questions or concerns."

This is why I recommend that you **Don't hide behind the keyboard.**

DON'T HIDE BEHIND THE KEYBOARD TO DELIVER BAD NEWS

Instead, consider flipping the script. If you've got to be the bearer of bad tidings to your client, I recommend the following steps.

- Reach out to your client via email and arrange a time for a brief chat (sooner rather than later).
- During this call, explain the situation and its implications.
- Then, pivot toward potential solutions to alleviate the negative impact.

- Finally, follow up with a report outlining the developments and strategies discussed during the call.

While the initial conversation might be uncomfortable, your client will likely appreciate your honesty, not to mention talking through the issues can make it easier to come to solutions. By making the call, they'll hear your comforting voice and be able to brainstorm with you in real time.

This approach is especially valuable in an era where real-time conversations are becoming increasingly rare.

TIP 22

Go Back to Move Forward

*A*ll attorneys know the feeling of receiving a new case.

- The rush of excitement.
- The sense of responsibility.
- The brainstorming and development of strategy.

Typically, these assignments are delivered via email, brimming with attachments that provide background information about the incident, including file notes, reports, and perhaps a demand letter or complaint.

However, amid this flurry of information, one document often gets overlooked despite its paramount importance: the attorney assignment letter or, in certain cases, the retention agreement. This letter lays out several critical aspects of the counsel's representation of the client. It specifies the exact name of the client, the scope of representation, applicable insurance coverages, initial procedural requests or directives, and reporting requirements.

As the case progresses, attorneys naturally focus on each new development, always looking ahead. In this forward momentum, the significance of the assignment letter might seem to diminish over time. But those attorneys who are truly client-focused understand that this letter is a treasure trove of essential information that needs to be referenced regularly. That's what I mean when I say, **Go back to move forward.**

In other words, the assignment letter or retention agreement isn't just our starting point. It's our *anchoring point.* It's the foundation upon which *all* else is based. If we don't go back and reference it with each major step, we run the risk of getting off track on even the most basic points of representation.

In my practice, I've observed attorneys making all types of preventable, embarrassing mistakes just by not following this principle. Some examples are listed below:

- Entering for an improperly named client,
- Failing to follow strategic directives,
- Hiring the wrong court reporting service,
- Missing reporting deadlines,
- Retaining experts without authorization, and
- Filing unapproved pleadings.

THE ASSIGNMENT LETTER IS A BEACON

Remember, the client has invested time and effort into clearly laying out their expectations and instructions in the assignment letter or retention agreement. Don't let the hectic pace of litigation make you lose sight of them. Make it a point to revisit the assignment letter or retention agreement routinely. It is a resource that can guide you through the complexities of your case, helping you meet your client's expectations, and avoid potential pitfalls.

TIP 23

Don't Always Cite to the Record

As attorneys, we're trained to include citations as early and as often as possible.

It's a practice we tend to apply to almost any filing or submission.

Each assertion we make about the case is typically accompanied by a reference, whether it's a complaint paragraph, deposition page and line number, or plaintiff's interrogatory response number. Similarly, when we present a legal standard, it is immediately followed by the relevant statutory provision, case citation, treatise, or restatement section. In federal court, if the opinion to which we're citing is unpublished, we even attach the whole dang thing to the motion itself!

This approach not only ensures that we're communicating our clients' stance effectively, but also demonstrates our thorough review of the case file before penning a single word. It signals to the court that our arguments are well-grounded and carefully deliberated, and our averments are rounded in the evidentiary record, which dispels any accusations of half-hearted advocacy.

All true. All legitimate. But not all the time.

Don't always cite to the record.

Let me explain.

When we're advocating *for* the client, yes, we do need to cite to the record. But when it comes to case reporting *to* the client, we need to rethink this strategy or run the risk of offending those very same folks: our clients.

As attorneys, we've all been there. It goes something like this: You request a directive, authority, or approval from the client during a conference call or in a status report. As litigation progresses and it's time for another client update, you realize that they haven't yet responded to your prior request.

The nerve! Don't they know how long you've waited? Your prior request is clearly documented, perhaps even underlined.

I'm loath to admit that at the outset of my career, there were times when I remember writing something like: "Per the attached report, we are reiterating our request for . . . " and then I would proceed to "cite to the record," meaning I would point out the previous client reporting in the matter. Not my best moment(s). In my defense, I didn't see the problem with it at the time. I do now.

CITE THE RECORD FOR THE CLIENT, NOT TO THE CLIENT

Attorneys must always consider how their communication will be perceived by their clients. It's presumptuous to assume a lack of response indicates oversight. The client may be internally deliberating on the matter or merely waiting for certain developments before committing to a litigation strategy.

Even if they genuinely forgot your request, wouldn't that be understandable? They are human, juggling *many* more claims than the number of cases we handle.

If a response is still pending, it's entirely appropriate to ask again. If there is no response over the course of several reports, politely request a time to chat briefly. Of course, if the directive is required by a particular deadline, which is fast approaching, then a more aggressive policy may need to be employed.

However, there's no need to highlight that it's a repeated request. Regardless of the reason, there's no scenario I can see in which that approach ends well. Unlike submissions to the court, leave the citations out of it.

TIP 24

Always Offer a Draft

*Y*ou're absolutely positive that everything between the four corners of each page is perfect. After all, you've written it. Cue the self-important music.

You've penned it meticulously, cross-referenced each citation, and proofread it seven times over. Two colleagues have reviewed and praised your work, reinforcing your confidence. You file it, supremely confident that the judge will be swayed by your argument.

There's only one problem. Your client hasn't even laid eyes on it.

Maybe that's not a problem. But maybe it is. Maybe that oversight will come back to bite both of you. Thus, the next tip is to **Always offer a draft.**

THE DANGER OF ASSUMING

It's an unfortunate practice among attorneys. We tend to submit filings without client approval. We sometimes think that once we get the authority to file, the client's involvement ends. That's tantamount to forgetting for whom we are working.

- We assume that, once we've talked with the client generally about the filing, and gone over the pros and cons, anticipated cost, effect on potential resolution, and predicted result, we're cleared to go.
- We assume that since the filing is brimming with factual details and legal intricacies, our client wouldn't want to take the time to read it. (After all, don't they trust us? Wasn't it their choice to hire us in the first place?)

Therein lies the problem: we *assume*.

The main issue here is the lack of choice. If the client doesn't want to read it, that's fine; at least offer them the *option* to decline.

THE CLIENT'S PERSPECTIVE

We can become overly engrossed in the case at hand, striving to position it for the best possible outcome. We believe our motion advances an argument that strengthens our defense or could potentially dismiss our client from the matter entirely.

However, our clients often see beyond what's immediately in front of them. They understand that once the arguments are filed on the public docket, their names, reputations, and brands are eternally linked with our words. This could have unintended repercussions that we might not have considered. Many times, we *couldn't* have considered them because we don't even know about them. These issues can be avoided simply by taking one extra step and letting the client double-check our work.

So, instead of submitting your work without your client's input, ask them how far in advance they'd like to review your draft. Some may opt not to see it at all, but the offer at least demonstrates respect for their role in the process. Once you get your client's internal deadline, calendar it and get to work.

Those who wish to review it typically request it one week prior to the deadline. When sending the draft, offer to discuss it over the phone and provide your availability. If they request changes, track your modifications and communicate them via email comments.

Remember, having the authority to *draft* does not equate to having the authority to *file*. There is typically no unconditional trust or complete autonomy. Always involve your client in the process. It is *their* case after all.

TIP 25

Do or Do Not.
There Is No Try.

*H*ere's another *Star Wars* reference. I know you've been patiently waiting.

Before everyone was enamored with Baby Yoda, there was . . . just plain old Yoda. During his first (by year of release) appearance in *The Empire Strikes Back*, Yoda imparted crucial wisdom to a young Luke Skywalker. Among the most poignant nuggets of advice, and one which has often adorned posters, bumper stickers, and memes alike is one I'll repeat here: **Do or do not. There is no try.**

When Luke was challenged to use the Force to lift his X-Wing out of a Dagobah swamp, he told Yoda that he'd "try." Yoda's response was this stern, uncompromising directive. He essentially told Luke not to simply exert a bit of effort and then give up. Instead, he should go all in; if it turned out to be mentally or physically impossible, then he realistically couldn't do it. But settling for a middle ground was not an option.

This is a valuable truth that attorneys should adopt when dealing with their clients. If a lawyer is doing their job properly, and if early resolution isn't in the cards, they must leave no stone unturned to protect their client's interests. Part of effective lawyering is possessing the mental dexterity to consider all angles, anticipate the opposition's strategy, and dig up facts relevant to the matter.

ASSUME IT WILL BE HARD

Few legal paths are entirely devoid of significant obstacles, even those that seem straightforward. For instance, consider the supposedly simple task of taking a non-party witness deposition. In a perfect world, it should be as easy as looking up the potential deponent's address or phone number, contacting them to appear voluntarily, sending a subpoena, and then conducting the deposition.

For some reason, attorneys think that the witness will respond with, "Sure, I'll take time out of my day to be grilled by lawyers under intense scrutiny. Why wouldn't I?!"

Ask any assigned counsel how often that happens. Here's a hint: you're more likely to do the Kessel Run in less than twelve parsecs.

In these situations, attorneys often find themselves ignored or snubbed by potential deponents, struggling to find accurate addresses, receiving returned mailings, and handling uncooperative responses. That's just the beginning. Next, they may face a no-show witness, necessitating a motion to enforce the subpoena, obtaining a court order (possibly against the other attorney's objections), and serving it on the witness. Even after all these hurdles, the deposition might still not take place. Consider the immense amount of time, effort, and money expended to make this ostensibly minor event happen.

THERE IS NO TRY

Here's the thing: the client doesn't want to hear about how tough it's been for you. They don't need to know about every painstaking task you've undertaken to depose a witness. They simply want to know that it *is* done, or when it *will* be done. Alternatively, if there's an insurmountable obstacle, like the witness passing away or the court denying your motion to compel the deposition, they want to be informed that it *physically cannot* be done.

What they don't want to hear is that the attorney "tried," but found it too difficult and gave up.

Listen to Yoda. Yoda is wise. Just look at the wonders it did for Luke.

When he listened, of course.

TIP 26

Sometimes, Work for Free

*W*hen I was a new associate, I once asked another attorney if I could, or should, voluntarily cut a billing entry. I reasoned that since the work I performed ended up being negated by an unexpected development, the client shouldn't have to pay for it.

The curt response to my inquiry was: "We don't work for free."

On its face, this policy seems entirely understandable. After all, I had put a lot of effort into this task. And at the time I did the work, we thought we would need the resulting product. However, the procedural posture of the matter had changed, and I knew my draft would never see the light of day, so billing the client just didn't sit right with me.

And for that reason, neither did this attorney's response.

Many attorneys adhere strictly to the rule of billing 0.1 for every six minutes they spend on a case, down to the exact millisecond. This is true irrespective of the task, the case, the client or, crucially, the value added. Every moment is accounted for meticulously, with their eyes fixed on the clock and fingers poised to record their time.

That certainly is one way to go about things. But I would encourage counsel to take a far less rigid approach: **Sometimes, work for free.**

Sometimes. Not *all* the time.

IT'S GOOD CUSTOMER SERVICE

I'm not suggesting that we should frequently absorb significant amounts of time. Like anyone else, we perform our duties with the expectation of payment, which necessitates billing our clients. Since my wife and I have been blessed with our first child, six-minute increments mean a lot more to me now than ever before.

However, I propose the incorporation of an element of customer service into our practices.

Let's put the shoe on the other foot for a moment. Think about some instances when you were "comped" for a good or service. Undoubtedly, on some of these occasions, there was an honest mistake made, and you were made whole through the waiver of a bill. But I'll also venture to guess that there were other times when nothing was wrong *per se*, but you were still offered something for either a discount or completely free, just because it seemed "right."

Didn't that feel good? Didn't that engender positive feelings toward the company or individual?

So why should attorneys' time be any different?

FREE TIME IS NOT LOST TIME

I remember a case where I had to undertake some preliminary research on a fairly complex preemption issue. Within a week of that research, following several rounds of negotiation, the case ended up settling.

Despite this, I opted not to bill my time for the research. I informed my client about a key piece of insight learned and mentioned that I hadn't billed for my time spent on it.

You know what? That non-billed time wasn't lost time, nor was the research wasted. It's useful information that both my client and I will have in our respective pockets for the next time a similar situation comes up.

But more importantly, billing the client for that time just didn't seem fair. And my client was very appreciative of my willingness to cut my costs.

And what's *fair* and *right* will always trump any amount of money we can make.

TIP 27

Assess and Request Early

$\int$imply put, early assessment leads to better preparation and often quicker resolution of a case. But making an early assessment also requires having all the relevant information upfront. That's why I offer this bit of advice for assigned counsel: **Assess and request early.**

One of the things I appreciate about our firm is our ability to assess new cases quickly. This early assessment also enables us to consider possible early resolutions. To accomplish this, we prioritize our investigative efforts right from the outset.

Some of these efforts we can obviously do on our own. We carry out extensive online searches, submit right-to-know requests, serve subpoenas, and both informally and formally solicit information and documentation from the plaintiff's counsel through discovery requests. However, one vital component that remains beyond our direct control is our clients' internal materials. And that's where the request comes in.

THE OBVIOUS AND THE NOT-SO-OBVIOUS

The importance of some client materials is self-explanatory. For example, the client might have any of the following:

- Incident reports,
- Photographs and videos of the incident or its aftermath,
- Minutes from post-incident safety meetings, and
- Statements about the occurrence.

If these materials exist, it's clear that assigned counsel needs them in order to complete a comprehensive analysis. For instance, a video might either corroborate or contradict the claimant's allegations, or perhaps an employee of our client witnessed the event and drafted a statement.

However, there may be other documentation that could significantly affect liability, for example:

- Perhaps an employee involved in an incident may have a history of reprimands for failure to adhere to the client's policies and procedures.
- The client may have a lackluster training curriculum that failed to address the circumstances underlying an accident.
- There may be a host of other claims against our client for the same kind of incident.
- The client may have failed to warn against a known danger.
- The client may have failed to preserve equipment in its post-incident condition.

Any of these scenarios, while unfavorable for liability defense, are still crucial factors in our analysis and affect our ability to provide an accurate assessment of a claim upon receipt.

JUST ASK FOR IT

Given the time-sensitive nature of our work, we attorneys need to include as many detailed requests to the client as possible in our initial reporting. Experienced attorneys will be able to promptly determine what requests need to be made. For example, a negligence case will typically need a slightly different set of materials as opposed to a strict product liability case.

But the key is to make sure the client receives as complete a list as possible, as early as possible. This will allow them time to search, identify, and compile everything (which often requires input from several different individuals in many different departments) in a timely manner.

The quicker and more comprehensive these requests are made, the sooner we and our client will both receive clarity regarding the valuation of a claim.

Know (and Be Honest About) Thine Enemy

*I*n *The Art of War*, Sun Tzu wrote, "If you know the enemy and know yourself, you need not fear the result of a hundred battles."

That's certainly the type of clarity being sought by our clients. Whether or not it is included in counsel's initial reporting, the question invariably remains in the mind of the client:

"How good is your opponent?"

In other words, how experienced is the other party's legal representative or team?

It's no surprise why they're asking. If the opposing counsel is known for their diligence, toughness, and experience, clients understand that the litigation journey will be challenging and intense. In such instances, the valuation of the claim implicitly increases, even though it may not be expressly stated.

Alternatively, if the opposing attorney is less "polished," clients may expect *their* counsel to control the litigation process, consequently reducing the claim's valuation.

My advice here is simple: **Know (and be honest about) thine enemy.**

HONESTY IS KEY

The client is just looking for an honest assessment. Unfortunately, attorneys don't always provide one. There are two reasons for this, *neither* of which is acceptable.

Reason One: Counsel simply doesn't know enough about the opposing counsel.

This excuse essentially amounts to willful ignorance with a splash of poor work ethic, and it should be dismissed out of hand. If the attorney has never litigated against this particular opponent before, they should ask around at their own firm. If that doesn't work, they call contacts from other firms. *Someone* they know will have information.

If these avenues prove unfruitful, they can seek information through defense listservs or other organizations. In a worst-case scenario, or to supplement previously gathered data, they can conduct an online search, including trial appearances and jury verdicts.

But *under no circumstances* should assigned counsel ever write: "Despite our best efforts, we have absolutely no idea about our opponent's experience or ability." Not to put too fine a point on it, but ignorance isn't an excuse, and the client knows it.

As problematic as the first reason is, the second is even more reprehensible.

Reason Two: Defense counsel knowingly over- or under-sells their opponent's skill level for personal, selfish reasons.

Counsel may believe that if they accurately report that their opponent is a formidable foe, the client will deem them as overmatched. Or conversely, if they, again, accurately, inform their client that the plaintiff's counsel is a pushover, the client will have unrealistic expectations and set the bar too high with respect to a result.

Not only is this practice deceitful, but it also shows that the attorney either does not trust their own abilities, or that they don't trust the client to be objective in receiving and analyzing information about the opposition.

None of this is good. And all of it is very easily avoidable. If you don't know your enemy, find out about them. Find out who they are and how good they are. Then give an honest answer to your client. They will appreciate it and understand.

Even more importantly, when they're properly informed about the opposition, they do not need to *fear the result of a hundred battles*, let alone a single legal case.

TIP 29

Hit "Send"
Before Hitting the Road

The pandemic fundamentally changed the way we travel for work.

Initially, industries were a bit shell-shocked. We hadn't ever experienced something like this before. And yet, slowly but surely and, in many cases, very impressively, the world adopted the word "remote."

This is certainly true for attorneys. Compared to other professions, we were very fortunate to be able to transition to remote work fairly easily. Depositions, hearings, and mediations all took place over Zoom. Many still do.

Was it new? Yes. Did it produce some unforgettable moments? Absolutely.

"I'm not a cat," anyone? (Google it if you haven't seen it.)

But now we're gradually getting back to in-person events. And for counsel, that often means traveling for work. Which, after years of being cooped up, understandably elicits feelings of excitement.

But lest we get ahead of ourselves, here's my next tip: **Hit "Send" before hitting the road.**

In other words, before assigned counsel gets back on the road, we need to slow down and take a minute to email the client for approval.

GIVE THE CLIENT OPTIONS

Granted, for some case events, there really is no choice. If a court has gone back to in-person oral arguments, attorneys must attend. However, when options are available, clients should be informed about all aspects of potential trips.

Consider a situation where a mediation could be held either virtually or in person. It's important to present clients with the pros and cons of each option. For instance, if you and your client attend a mediation virtually, time and money associated with travel will be saved. Conversely, meeting the plaintiff in person to present your liability defenses and planned motion practice might be impactful, and may increase your chances of settling the case.

The same principle applies when scheduling a deposition. Perhaps you want to gauge the plaintiff's body language in person or have them examine physical exhibits. Again, it may or may not be beneficial. While you can certainly provide your recommendation, the final decision should rest with the client.

A PERSONAL EXAMPLE

Here is a real-life illustration of this point. I once received notices for three virtual depositions from a plaintiffs' counsel for employees of my corporate client, all scheduled for the same day. Upon discussing the matter with the insured, they expressed comfort in having me present with them due to the identities of the deponents, as well as the sheer number of anticipated exhibits. I sought permission from the claims adjuster, providing detailed reasoning, as well as estimated costs for my time and travel expenses. She responded quickly with her approval and thanked me for contacting her rather than simply making the drive.

Would anyone have been upset if I had made the choice unilaterally? Maybe so, maybe not. And not that long ago, it wouldn't even have been a question, because in-person was the only option. But it's a new, changed world. When there are options available, it's common courtesy to defer to the client.

As the world reopens, clients understand that professional travel is once again an option, and sometimes even a necessity. Just give them the opportunity to make an informed decision before you head out the door.

TIP 30

Think About Someone Else for a Change

*A*ttorneys can be . . . dare I say . . . a bit rigid. We focus on what's required of us and when.

This is not just confined to court submissions but extends to client reporting as well. After all, we are inherently rule-based creatures who thrive within the confines provided to us. We're given the parameters of tasks, and we complete them.

That's actually a good trait for attorneys, not a bad one. If you recall from a previous tip, I suggested that we keep referring back to the client's assignment letter or retention agreement. It's the roadmap for assigned counsel. These requirements are painstakingly assembled, and each line is included for a reason. Keeping to that roadmap is how we get things done well.

But every so often, we need to take off the blinders and take a broader view. We need to ask ourselves why the reporting rules are there in the first place. Why do our clients need us to submit certain information at certain times?

- Is it just to make our lives a bit harder?
- Or because each case we litigate is just *that* fascinating?
- Or maybe they want to test our reading comprehension skills?

Actually, it's none of the above. The truth is much simpler. These reporting guidelines exist because *the claims handler or client representative is also reporting to someone.*

IT'S NOT JUST ABOUT YOU

Your client perceives their internal superior similarly to how you view your client, creating a chain of duties that must be met. So, the pressure you feel when you are required to send a report, adhering to certain guidelines and timelines, mirrors the stress your client faces when they consider reporting up the chain in their organization. In other words, your client's ability to fulfill their responsibilities hinges on your ability to meet yours.

This leads to my final tip: **Think about someone else for a change.**

KEEP THE LARGER GOAL IN MIND

As attorneys, particularly assigned counsel, we're all about parameters, and that's what makes us good at what we do. But the rules aren't an end to themselves; they're a means to an end. Our clients rely on us to follow the parameters of our tasks as part of fulfilling a larger goal. Remembering this inspires us to do our jobs better, and even to go the extra mile when necessary.

So do your job, not *just* because a document tells you to, but because your client relies on you. You owe it to them to deliver.

Put yourself in the client's shoes and remember what they're up against.

In my view, that's what has been lacking in the profession for some time now.

And that's what makes the difference between good attorneys and great ones.

Epilogue

$\mathcal{A}$s we conclude, I'd like to revisit the core question I presented in the Introduction to this book: *How can we, as attorneys, better serve our clients?*

All the tips I've shared in these pages are helpful practices I've picked up along the way, whether from my own experiences (including mistakes) or those of others. But at their heart, they all are different ways of answering that one, simple question.

And that's important, because I think that, without having that core question constantly before me, I never would have thought to adopt these tips in my own practice.

In other words, the tips throughout this book presented themselves to me organically *because I was asking that question in the first place.*

So, the last thing I'd like to leave with you is this: *Keep asking that question.* Keep it as your top priority. When you are litigating a case, the little bird on your shoulder should keep asking how each and every email, call, motion, inspection, and other step is serving the client.

Obviously, I believe putting these tips into practice will make us all better, more effective attorneys, but they are by no means the end-all-be-all of how to be a great attorney.

As long as you are constantly seeking to serve your own clients better, I believe other answers to this question will come to you, as well.

For me, I know I'm going to keep asking the question. The tips in the preceding pages are just a few of the answers I've found . . . for now.

About the Author

Nate R. Bohlander, Esq. is a Partner with Morgan, Akins & Jackson, PLLC, as well as chair of the firm's National Aviation Practice Group. He is licensed in Pennsylvania, New York and New Jersey, and works out of the firm's Philadelphia office. Nate regularly defends airlines, product manufacturers, construction organizations, commercial trucking companies, and many other businesses in a wide range of civil suits. He lives in the woods with his wife, daughter, and golden retriever.